To Zoe and Sigurd
— F.T.

First American Edition 2020
Kane Miller, A Division of EDC Publishing
P.O. Box 470663, Tulsa, OK 74147-0663
www.kanemiller.com
Text by Harriet Evans
Text copyright © Caterpillar Books Ltd 2020
Illustrations copyright © Fotini Tikkou 2020
Library of Congress Control Number: 2019952237
ISBN: 978-1-68464-056-0
Printed in China
CPB/1400/1387/0320
10 9 8 7 6 5 4 3 2 1

FAMILY HEROES

Keeping Things Going

Illustrated by Fotini Tikkou

Kane Miller
A DIVISION OF EDC PUBLISHING

My parents serve the public,

make the world a better place.

And when they can help others,

they will, in every case.

My mommy is an officer, she works for the police.

She leads patrols on horseback,

and helps to keep the peace.

My daddy is a teacher,
he helps us learn new things.
And with his endless patience,
enjoys what each day brings.

My mommy is a volunteer, she helps people far away.

Whatever problem, big or small,

I know she'll save the day.

My daddy is a lifeguard, he taught me how to swim.

Bobbing on the ocean waves,

I know I'm safe with him.

My mommy drives the school bus,
she makes sure we're never late.
She's always kind to new kids,
the students think she's great.

My daddy is a firefighter, determined and so brave.

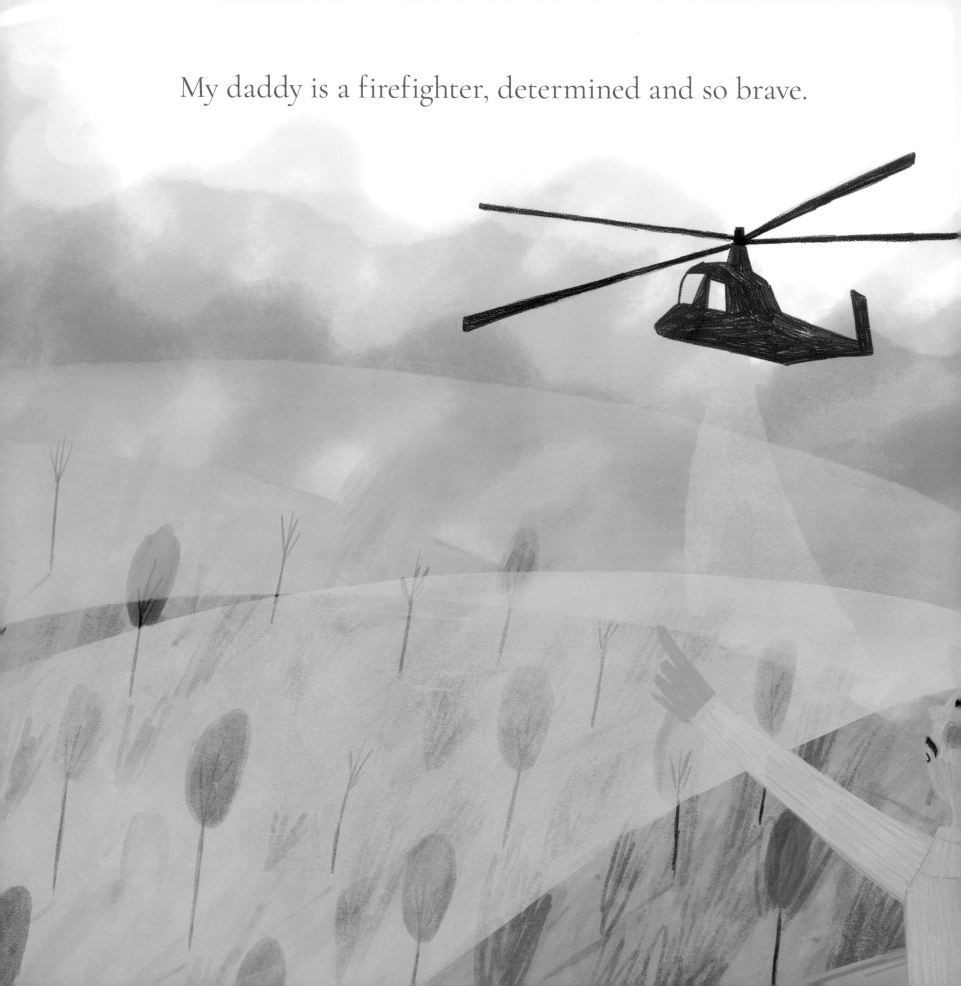

When he's in his shiny truck,

his mission is to save.

My mommy is a mail carrier:

letters, parcels, cards, and gifts.

She helps them travel safely,

working hard on all her shifts.

My daddy drives a tow truck

for when vehicles break down.

He comes right to the rescue,

and takes them back to town.

My mommy's always busy, she helps out those in need.

Wherever there's a problem,

she'll get there at great speed.

My daddy is a ranger,
 and he patrols the park.

He likes protecting nature,
and works from dawn till dark.

My parents serve the public,

make the world a better place.

And when they can help others,

they will, in every case.